May God
bless you beyond
in your every endeavor
Always
Jacobia ♡

Unless otherwise indicated, all Old and New Testament Scriptures quotations are taken from the New King James Version of the Bible.

Scriptures quotations marked KJV are taken from the King James Version of the Bible.

Unless otherwise indicated, all Old and New Testament Scriptures quotations are taken from the *Amplified Bible*.

Manuscript and Project by Ladalia Postell
Diamond Graphics by Emmanuel Johnson
Front & Back Cover Photographs by Reggie Baker (HMC Photographer)
Front & Back Cover Designed by Flo's Productions
Website: http://flosproductions.nstemp.biz
Email: florencedyer@comcast.net
810.624.3660

ISBN 0-9769645-2-X

Saying It With Poetry

Saying It With Poetry
Expressions From the Heart

By
Ladalia Postell

FLO'S PRODUCTIONS PUBLISHING SERVICE
An Affiliate of Writers & Self Publishers Association

Genesee County

A Word From The Publisher

Along our journey in life we come across an uncommon person. It is up to us to truly recognize that we have been divinely setup by the Master. This is how I recognized my encounter with Ladalia. It has been truly a blessing publishing her awesome poetry. *Ladalia's poetic artistry is a true reflection of who God is and what He is in her life.*

–Florence Dyer
Owner of FLO'S PRODUCTIONS
Author/Publisher/Graphic Designer

FORWARD

Although I dabbled with rhyme as early as grade school, and often used poetry as a teaching tool during my career as an elementary school teacher; my true passion for poetry was seriously triggered well into my career as a Therapist and Medical Social Worker. I suppose one could say the tasks of conveying the most crucial messages came much easier for me through poetic phrases. It became clear to me that my writing skills far outweighed my verbal. Consequently, "Saying It With Poetry" became an instrument through which I have been better able to express my thoughts and feeling of love, happiness, joy, and sorrow.

It is my sincere hope that my expressions will, in some way, speak to the needs of the reader; whether it is for consolation, inspiration, spirituality, or just the sheer enjoyment of poetic rhyme.

Ladalia
A. Postell

Author

ABOUT THE AUTHOR

Ladalia Ann Postell was born in Albany, Georgia. She attended the public schools of Albany, and graduated at the tender age of sixteen. She attended Albany State College, now University, and obtained a B.A. degree in Sociology, with a minor in Elementary Education. Ladalia was only nineteen when she began her teaching career at her Alma Mater, Monroe High School, where she taught six years before relocating to Columbus, Georgia, and teaching first grade at Dexter Elementary School at Fort Benning Military Base.

Ladalia was married at age twenty, and blessed with a son, Robert J. Griffin Jr., who has further blessed her with two beautiful grandchildren, Arianna Ladalia, and Robert III.

In the middle seventies, Ladalia relocated to Flint, Michigan, where she completed an Addiction Studies Program at Hurley Medical Center; after which she worked as a Substance Abuse Therapist at Insight Inc. for twenty years. During the course of her career at Insight, she acquired a Masters Degree in Social Work from the University of Michigan in Ann Arbor. She is presently employed at Hurley Medical Center (a level I Trauma Center) as a Medical Social Worker in the Emergency Room.

Ladalia is a faithful member of Grace Emmanuel Baptist Church in Flint, Michigan under the guidance of Pastor Marvin A. Jennings, Sr. She loves the Lord and is inspired by His word.

ACKNOWLEDGEMENTS

First, and foremost I give glory and honor to my Lord and Savior Jesus Christ. I thank Him for the gift of poetic expression.

There are a number of special people to whom I would like to give thanks for their encouragement and continuous support of me in compiling and publishing this, my first book.

To my Parents, whose love and support has always made me feel I can do anything if it is according to God's will.

To my son Rob, who has been an enormous blessing to me from the day of his birth.

To my sister, Gwendolyn, who is always there for me for whatever I need.

A special thanks to my Disciplemaker, Deborah McNeal, who has been most supportive and instrumental to my Spiritual growth.

To Myra Davis, whose encouragement gave me the extra push to contact a publisher.

MY LIFE PURPOSE

I.   *To serve the Lord in all that I do and
      say.*

II.   *To use my spiritual gifts, heart, abilities,
      personality,
      Experiences to help others.*

III. *To be more like Jesus. (gentle, kind,
      compassionate, loving,
      giving, forgiving, humble, trustworthy,
      truthful, dependable, and dedicated to
      do God's will.)*

CONTENTS

9

I

Spirituality in Rhyme

I thank and praise God for the gift of poetry. It is only by His grace that poetic rhyme flows within me. I recognize this talent as a gift because I realize that I am nothing, and can do nothing without my Creator, Protector, and Savior. The following poems were inspired by my firm belief in God, His son Jesus, and His Holy Spirit, who lives inside of me.

NO GREATER LOVE

No greater love could there ever be,
Than the love that Jesus has for you and me.
He suffered, died, and was buried you see,
So that you and I could all be free.

Not a mumbling word did he speak;
No escape did He ever seek.
He suffered, died, and was buried you see,
So the enemy of man would know defeat.

I thank Him for his sacrifice.
He was persecuted, beaten, and crucified.
Yes, He suffered, died, and was buried you see,
No greater love could there ever be.

Thank God He is risen, and will forever be
A beacon of hope for the world to see.
For He suffered, died, and was buried you see;
And there's no greater love that could ever be.

CHANGE

Everything in this world,
We can expect to change.
Only our Lord and Savior,
Will forever remain the same.

The same yesterday, today, and forever,
Our Master's promises are true.
He is our Rock and our Salvation,
And He will always see us through.

As the world around us changes,
On one thing we can depend.
Jesus never changes,
And His mercies never end.

Our Savior never slumbers nor sleeps,
And He knows our every need.
He has not, does not, and will not change.
He is an awesome God indeed.

May you rest in the assurance of God's unchanging love.

GOD'S SPECIALTY

It does not matter how rough the road;
Or what you are going through.
You have a Savior who specializes
In giving love and saving you.

The darkest days are brightened
By His mercy and His grace.
He took our sins upon himself;
Suffered and died for the human race.

What an awesome God we serve;
No other can compare.
Our God specializes in love
And delivering us from despair.

So never doubt the Word of God.
His promises are true and in that we can trust.
We serve a wonderful God who cannot fail,
And Hs specialty is loving and saving us.

May your days be brightened by this truth.
In Jesus' Name

Amen

JESUS

Just the mentioning of His name
Brings joy and eases so much pain.
Jesus, our Savior and our friend;
His love and compassion have no end.

When the world seems to be getting us down,
And out smiles have turned into frowns;
We need only to praise His name,
And concentrate on the reason He came.

Let us praise Jesus every morning,
And give Him praises throughout each day.
Let us never cease to call His name
And look to Him to show us the way.

Jesus is our Lord and Savior,
He is our all and all.
There is so much power in His name,
And on Him we can always call.

Jesus, Jesus, Jesus,
The sweetest name I have ever heard.
Jesus, Jesus, Jesus,
What a mighty God we serve!

Let us bless the Lord at all times,
And His praises be continually in our mouths.

A MIGHTY LOVE

God looked down from heaven,
And saw us going astray.
So He sent His precious son Jesus,
To teach us and show us the way.

Jesus walked among us,
And paid the penalty for our sins.
He suffered, died, and was buried,
To ensure us a world without end.

What a mighty God we serve.
He is worthy of all our trust.
No greater love could there ever be,
Than what Jesus has for us.

The sacrifice He made;
Coming down from heaven above;
Taking all our sins upon Himself;
What a Mighty, Mighty, Love!

May we be forever mindful of God's love and sacrifice.

JESUS IS THE ANSWER

Could we even lift a finger,
If our Savior was not here?
Could we take a single breath,
If we were not in His care?

Is there anything we could do,
Or anything we could feel?
Would we have awakened this morning,
Had it not been the Master's will?

Are we anchored in the Lord?
Is He the head of our life?
Or do we look to other sources
When we are faced with pain and strife?

Jesus is the answer!
He is everything we need.
He is the source of all our strength.
And He is a friend indeed.

There Is No Problem That Jesus Cannot Solve.

OUR BLESSED SAVIOR

We have a blessed Savior;
Jesus Christ is His name.
To deliver us from a world of sin,
Is the reason why He came.

We celebrate His coming,
To transfigure you and me.
And because of His saving power,
All who love Him have been set free.

We thank Jesus for His coming,
And His everlasting love.
He is our blessed Savior,
Sent to us from heaven above.

May The Joy And Peace Of His Coming,
Be With You Until He Comes Back Again.

THINGS ETERNAL I

What things are important in our lives today?
How often do we take the time to just kneel down and pray?
Do we concern ourselves with material things,
And burden ourselves with worry about what tomorrow will bring?

Are we overwhelmed with debt, and cannot sleep?
Do we agonize daily over what we should eat,
And spend hours deciding what clothes we will wear;
While neglecting the things for which Jesus wants us to care?

Are there subtle idols in our lives?
Do earthly treasures occupy our thoughts?
Do we seek pleasures that are not of God,
And ignore our sins, failures, and faults?

What are our first thoughts in the morning,
And our very last thoughts at night?
Are we focused on things eternal;
Walking by faith, and not by sight?

Let us not be deceived by Satan,
Who stalks us daily with temporal things.
We must stay focused on things eternal;
The love, peace, and joy that only Jesus brings.

My our hearts, souls, and minds, be continually focused on
THINGS ETERNAL.

THINGS ETERNAL II

This world is full of troubles;
Filled with things that will not last.
So many things that would distract us
From God's plan and our greatest tasks.

When our closest friends forsake us,
And we struggle with grief and pain,
We can look to God for comfort;
Our inner peace, He will sustain.

Nothing in this world is lasting,
And of that we can be sure.
We must hope for thing eternal;
God will help us to endure.

To love God with all our hearts,
Our souls, our strength, and minds,
Is all that really matters;
All else will be left behind.

This world is here but for a moment;
Like the dew, it will soon be gone.
We must keep our minds on things eternal,
And look forward to our Heavenly home.

May God help us to build our hopes on things eternal.

BLESSED ADVERSITY

As surely as we are born,
There will be storms in our lives.
Trials and tribulations
Are but blessings in disguise.

How so, you might ask,
Are we blessed by so much pain?
A very clear explanation
Can be found in the book of James.

A test of our faith,
And the opportunity to grow;
When we are faced with adversity,
Is when God's blessings flow.

God is closer during the storms,
Than at any other time.
His promise to never leave us,
Must be implanted in our minds.

So when we face adversities,
And our hearts are filled with pain;
It is then we must count our blessings,
And know God's love will sustain.

May God bless us with the wisdom and patience
to recognize and accept the blessings in adversity.

THE MIRROR

Lord, help us to reflect your love,
And be more like you in every way.
Let our thoughts be pure, and deeds be kind,
And your voice be heard in everything we say.

When we look in the mirror Lord,
Please help us to see
A clear reflection,
Of what you want us to be.

Let us seek your direction
In all that we do.
Let our mirrors reflect
A clear image of You.

We thank you Lord, for your guidance.

SPIRIT WORDS

Speak to us Lord, and show us the way.
Help us to hear clearly your words, and obey.
Give us the will to never cease to pray.
Let us speak only what you would have us to say.

Let us stay focused, and our hearts remain true.
Tell us clearly Lord, what you would have us to do.
And when we are confused about what to pursue;
Let us wait patiently for guidance from You.

Speak to us Lord, when troubles arise,
And the enemy is stalking and seeking our demise.
Let your Holy Spirit take control of our lives.
Keep us focused dear Lord; keep our eyes on the prize.

And when this life is over, and your will is completely done;
The enemy defeated, and the battle is won;
And the things of this world we have risen beyond;
Let us rejoice in the embrace of your precious son.

BEYOND THE VEIL

There was a barrier between man and God
Before God sent his son.
But when Jesus died on Calvary,
The barrier between us was torn.

The veil no longer separates us,
When we walk in sweet accord.
Jesus paved the way for us
To stand boldly before our Lord.

When Jesus closed his eyes in death,
He paid for all our sins.
He welcomed us beyond the veil,
And vowed to be our friend.

Trials and tribulations will surely come,
And sometimes we will surely fail.
But we need not worry, and never fear,
Jesus delivered us from the veil.

May we take comfort in knowing that Jesus'
Love has lifted us BEYOND THE VEIL.

ABIDING IN JESUS

Today I heard a message
That rang so very clear.
It filled my heart with gladness,
And took away my fear.

Because I abide IN Jesus,
And His words abide IN me;
I can ignore the antics of Satan,
Because my soul has been set free.

Many Christians walk WITH Jesus,
But fail to let Him IN.
When we are filled with His Holy Spirit,
We can more readily turn from sin.

We see through the eyes of Jesus
When IN Him we abide.
Our behavior will reflect His presence,
When IN us He resides.

May our behavior always reflect
Our lives in Jesus, and His presence in us.

SENIORS
WE ARE SO BLESSED

We are so blessed to celebrate
God's gift of senior years.
He has seen us through so many trials,
And dried so many tears.

God promised to never leave us,
And His promises are true.
We know that no matter what the problems
He will always see us through.

We thank God for His many blessings,
And we give Him all the praise.
He carried us when we could not walk,
And has kept us in His ways.

As we look back over the years,
We can see God's saving power.
We have learned to trust His saving grace,
Even in our darkest hours.

So we celebrate our Lord and Savior;
And we will give Him all our best.
For he loved us even before we were born;
And for that seniors, WE ARE SO BLESSED.

JESUS SMILES

Jesus smiles when we trust Him,
And He smiles when we give Him praise.
Jesus smiles when we serve Him,
And acknowledge Him in all our ways.

When we give our lives to Jesus,
We bring smiles upon His face.
We are blessed by His loving spirit,
As we enter this Holy place.

When we are burdened down with troubles,
And we can't seem to find our way;
Jesus smiles when we turn things over.
He will wash our sins away.

Jesus smiles when we trust Him,
And He smiles when we serve Him.
Jesus smiles when we love Him.
Let us all make Jesus smile.

May we be a disappointment to the enemy,
as we bring smiles to Jesus' face.

WHISPERS

Sweet whispers from our Savior,
Is what I long to hear.
When we stand still and listen,
His voice is always clear.

When we are burdened down with troubles,
And can't seem to find our way;
we can just stand still and listen
To what Jesus has to say.

He whispers so very gently,
And with such loving care.
When we take time to listen,
Cloudy days become oh so fair.

Stand still, look up, and listen;
You will hear the Master's voice.
Sweet whispers from our Savior
Give us reason to rejoice.

May God grant us the will to listen,
and heed His whispers of guidance and love.

WHEN WE PRAY

Often times when we kneel to pray,
We don't know what to say or how to say it.
Be not dismayed, for it is true,
That God sends to us, his Holy Spirit.

He listens to our hearts,
And hears just what we need;
Then stands before our Father,
And with groaning, He intercedes.

Our words need not be eloquent ,
Or lengthy when we pray.
Sometimes a simple Thank You,
Is all we need to say.

For God knows our every thought,
And hears our every plea.
So when we pray, we need not worry;
Mere earnestness is the key.

When we pray in earnest,
God hears our every word.
So we must keep on praying,
Because our prayers are always heard.

WE MUST FORGIVE

Matthew 18:22 tells us what to do
When troubles arise between me and you.
Forgiveness is proof of love
Which comes to us from Heaven above.

Jesus watches and prays with trust
That we forgive each other as He does us.

If we cannot find it in our hearts
To forgive each other here on earth;
How then, can we realize God's plan for us?

"Forgive us our trespasses,
As we forgive those who trespass against us,"
Are not just words we haphazardly say.
They should be written on our hearts,
And reflected in our ways.

So we must forgive each other,
Just as Jesus tells us to do.
For life is all about Jesus,
And not about me and you.

May we be filled with the spirit of God,
With love and forgiveness in our hearts.

THE SWEETEST NAME

All hail the power of Jesus' name.
It's the sweetest name I know.
The mentioning of it brings so much joy;
I will tell it wherever I go.

Jesus, my Savior and my King.
Jesus, I will let Your praises ring.

Jesus, a shelter from every storm.
Jesus, what wonders You perform.

Jesus, my Master and the Prince of Peace.
Jesus, Your grace and mercy never cease.

Jesus, the Way, the Truth, and the Light.
Jesus, let me be pleasing in Your sight.

Jesus, no sweeter name shall there ever be.
Jesus, we thank you for setting our souls free.

Amen

ABUNDANT GIVING

God assures us that when we freely give,
There will be great rewards.
With blessings to meet our every need,
His grace, He will always impart.

There are so many blessings,
That come with the joy of giving.
It is when we freely give,
That we experience abundant living.

The way to Abundant Living is Abundant Giving.

BETTER SERVANTS

Use us Lord, help us do your will.
Teach us your ways and help us obey.
Lead us and guide us,
And not let us stray.

Renew our minds,
So that it is stayed on you.
Let our words be kind,
Necessary and true.

Give light to our lives Lord,
With the truth of your word.
And let us be beacons
To some soul who has not heard.

Let your goodness and your glory
Be reflected in all our ways.
Let us praise you, and serve you
For the rest of our days.

Use us dear Lord.
Have your way in our lives.
Deliver us from the enemy,
And keep our eyes on the prize.

May the Lord use us to be better servants to His will.

HE HAS SET ME FREE

When I was six I can recall
My grandmother saying to me:
"Love the Lord with all your heart,
Because He has set you free."

By age sixteen, I knew the Lord.
And was inspired by His Holy Word.
I knew He was watching over me,
By the many sermons that I heard.

As the years progressed,
And God kept blessing me,
I grew stronger in His ways.
By age thirty I rededicated myself to Him
And knew I'd walk with Him the rest of my days.

There was a time in my forties,
When it was so very clear
That God was carrying me.
The road was rough and the going so tough,
But He blessed me beyond degree.

And now I stand before you,
Anchored in the Lord with not a single doubt;
That no matter what the problems may be,
My God will surely bring me out.

When my granddaughter Arianna Ladalia was six, I said to her,
Just what my grandmother said to me:
"Love the Lord with all your heart,
Because He has set you free.

GOD'S WILL, NOT OURS

God knows all about us;
Even better than we know ourselves.
He knows our every need,
And hears our daily prayers.

When we go to God in prayer,
There is one thing we must understand.
It is His will, not ours, that must be done.
So we must leave it all in His capable hands.

We can pray with confidence
That God hears us and He cares.
And even when it seems He is far away,
We can be sure that He is always near.

Let us not be impatient when we pray,
Because God is never late.
His answers may be one of three;
Yes, No, or Wait.

So when we kneel again in prayer,
Let us not forget to say:
Father let your will be done.
Have your way Lord, have your own way.

THE SOLID ROCK

When the storms of life are raging,
As they are certain to do;
We can call on the name of Jesus,
He never fails to see us through.

His love is everlasting,
And on Him we can depend.
Not only is He our Savior,
He is also our best friend.

So when the storms of life keep raging,
And Satan puts us to the test;
We need only to love and trust in Jesus,
And "little by little" He will do the rest.

Christ is the Solid Rock
On which we can always stand.
We need only to run to Him;
All power is in His hands.

May we never cease to praise God for His Son
Jesus,
The Solid Rock

OUR ADVOCATE, OUR FRIEND

We have a friend in Jesus;
In Him we can put our trust.
At the right hand of the Father,
He advocates for us.

With everything we do and say,
We want to please our Savior.
Because He bled and died for us,
And shows us so much favor.

We need not fret about anything;
Our Lord is in full control.
He watches even as we sleep,
With blessing waiting to unfold.

Yes, Jesus is our advocate;
And He is also our best friend.
We must praise Him without ceasing.
To Him be the glory....Amen.

LOOK UP

We have a Savior high above,
Who knows our every need.
He knows all about our troubles,
And never fails to intercede.

This world is full of trouble,
And God's children are not exempt.
But we need only to look up to Jesus,
And turn everything over to Him.

Don't be discouraged brothers and sisters,
When good works seem to go unnoticed.
You can be sure that Jesus cares,
And will reward every act of holiness.

When troubles surround us on every side,
And we can't seem to find our way;
We can look up and know that Jesus sees,
And hears us when we pray.

"Look up, there's nothing down but the ground"
Is my mother's favorite phrase.
And when we do, God is faithful
To lift us up, and brighten our days.

May God bless us to be able to Look Up,
And weather every storm.

MY HELP

Jesus is my help,
In all that I do and say.
He sent His Holy Spirit,
To guide me along the way.

Jesus is my help,
And so I have no fear.
I can live each day with peace of mind,
Because my Savior is always near.

Jesus is my help.
When I was lost and feeling down;
He lifted me up, and renewed my mind,
And turned my life around.

He provides my every need,
And hears me when I pray.
He keeps my feet on solid ground,
And will not let my stray.

Yes, Jesus is my help.
And in all my ways I will acknowledge Him,
And His will I will always do.
If you but let Him into your heart,
He will do the same for you.

We can boldly say: The Lord is my Helper.

NO NEED TO FEAR

We can trust in the Lord;
His promises are true.
No matter what the circumstance,
He will see us through.

We need not worry;
We need not fear.
Through every trial,
Our God is near.

He never slumbers;
Nor does He sleep.
He is the Good Sheppard
Who watches over His sheep.

We are His people, the sheep of His pasture.
He loves us without a doubt.
So there is no need for us to fear.
Trusting God shuts the enemy out.

May our faith and trust be increased,
And all fear is gone.

FORGIVENESS

God has said, "seek peace and pursue it";
And with that He will give us rest.
I asked Him to forgive my sins,
And strengthen me to pass life's tests.

Now I'm asking you dear Fran,
To forgive and to forget
The unrest that lies between us,
And the anger that I regret.

We are sisters in the Lord,
And He wants us to have joy;
And to do His will in everything,
So His blessings He can employ.

So let us not allow the enemy
To come in and steal our peace.
Let us love each other as God loves us,
And keep the enemy beneath our feet.

May God bless and keep you in His loving care.

OUR SHELTER

There is so much adversity
In this world today.
Many trials and tribulations
Are sure to come our way.

We can run to the arms of Jesus
When this world seems too much to bear.
In His arms He will hold us gently,
And will deliver us from despair.

Jesus is our shelter.
He is never far from us.
He shields us from the enemy,
And His promises we can trust.

There are demons all around us,
But we need not fret nor fear.
Jesus is our shelter,
And He is always near.

We Can Trust The Presence And The Power Of Jesus Always.

THE CHOICE

We have choices as to whom we will serve;
And the choices have been made clear.
We can choose God's son who came to save us,
Or the enemy who is out to destroy us.

The world was filled with darkness,
Before Jesus came on the scene.
The enemy was reigning victorious;
Thank God for the newborn king.

He was sent expressly to save us,
And deliver us from a world of sin.
So now the choice is ours,
As to who we will let be our friend.

If we choose to follow Jesus,
The reward is eternal life.
But if we choose the enemy,
The future is but pain and strife.

THE CHOICE IS OURS

May we choose to follow Jesus and be a
disappointment to the enemy.

ENCOURAGING WORDS

Our words carry enormous weight.
They can encourage or dismay.
We can build, or we can destroy,
By the words we choose to say.

God speaks clearly about the tongue;
And the damage it can do.
We must pray for guidance when we speak;
So that God's messages can shine through.

True, kind, and necessary,
Is what our words must be.
Testifying of His goodness,
Is what God wants of you and me.

He wants us to carry the message
Of His everlasting love.
And of His grace and mercy;
As He watches over us from Heaven above.

So go forth my brothers and sisters;
And speak with the gentleness of a dove.
Let us encourage one another;
And grow closer in Christian love.

May the words of our mouths be a disappointment to the enemy,
and bring a smile to the face of our Father.

PURPOSEFUL LIVING

God sent me by to tell you,
That he has a purpose for your life.
To be of service to His people
In their troubles and in their strife.

Have you ever asked the question,
My God, why am I here?
If you listen closely to the Master,
He makes our purpose clear.

To say we will pray for our brother
When he is experiencing hunger pains;
Is not fulfilling life's purpose.
And is far from spiritual gain.

We must forsake ourselves entirely,
And hear the cross of our fellowman.
If we are to have purposeful living,
And please God; we must take a stand.

So let us not neglect our purpose.
God smiles when we do His will.
Our thoughts, words, and deeds must all be kind;
So that our purpose for living is fulfilled.

May God grant each of us clear visions of our purpose for living;
And may our lives be an utter disappointment to the enemy.

THE WAY OUT

So much turmoil in the world today;
The enemy is truly on the move.
He is out to kill and destroy us all;
It is our souls he wants us to lose.

But there is a way out.

When we make the decision to live for Christ,
It is all the enemy needs,
To reinforce his plan to win our souls.
It is our weaknesses on which he feeds.

But there is a way out.

When we sing the Master's praises,
The enemy becomes outraged.
He steps up his forces of evil,
And goes on a violent rampage.

But there is a way out.

When we confess our sins, and kneel in prayer,
And commit to our Father's will;
The enemy's forces are at a loss,
Because then, our souls he cannot steal.

JESUS is the way out.

If we but call on the name of Jesus,
The enemy will have to flee.
There is so much power in His holy name;
No greater power could there ever be.

Yes, JESUS is the way out.

Because "greater is He that in you,
Than he that is in the world."
I John 4:4

THE GREAT INTERCESSOR

We have an intercessor,
His name is Jesus Christ.
He pleads relentlessly for our salvation;
And for that, He has paid the price.

He suffered, died, and was buried.
What greater love could there be?
Now He sits at the right hand of the Father,
Making intercessions for you and for me.

From the right hand of our Father,
Jesus knows our every need.
We need not ever worry;
He never fails to intercede.

So need we ask the question
What shall we do to be saved?
We need only to trust Jesus,
And the sacrifice that He made.

Because He lives and loves us so,
He forgives our every sin.
And frees us to go before the throne;
He is our Savior and our friend.

So we thank you Heavenly Father,
And we give you all the praise.
Thank you for the Great Intercessor;
Without whom we could not be saved.

THE PROMISE I

Did you ever think because you are a Christian,
You should be exempt from hardships and pain?
Have you wondered why sometimes
It seems your efforts are all in vain?

Have you wondered why some evil men
Seem to rise above life's tribulations?
And the harder you try, the more the enemy
Tries to steer you from salvation?

Have you ever tried to do your best,
And it just didn't turn out right?
Have you felt you just didn't have the strength,
And was tempted to give up the fight?

When the enemy is attacking you this way my friend;
There is one thing on which you can depend.
God's promise is not that we will not suffer,
But that He will be with us until the end.

He said He will never leave or forsake us;
And His promises are always true.
And although the road is sometimes rough,
God promised to take care of you.

Trust God to keep His promise, He is incapable of lying.

THE PROMISE II

"I will never leave thee, nor forsake thee,"
Is the promise our Master made.
And for that very reason,
We need never be afraid.

God is always standing by,
To ease our hurt and pain.
His promise to never leave us,
Will always remain the same.

We can boldly claim His promise,
As He watches us from His throne.
He sent His Holy Spirit
So we would never be alone.

In good times as well as bad,
We can trust God's Holy Word.
The promise of His presence
Is the sweetest truth I've ever heard.

We Can Trust God's Promise To Never Leave Or Forsake Us.

A FORGIVING SPIRIT

When I think of God's goodness,
And how He has set me free;
Forgiving others comes easy,
No matter what is done to me.

An unforgiving spirit
Is what the enemy loves.
Clinging to anger and bitterness
Blocks our blessings from Heaven above.

To let go and let God is the answer.
He forgives our every sin.
So we too, must forgive each other,
If Jesus is to be our friend.

Such joy comes with forgiveness.
It's been tested over and over again.
But we cannot expect God's forgiveness,
If we can't forgive our fellowman.

So let us pray for A Forgiving Spirit,
With love for friends and enemies too.
We must forgive those who offend us,
Just as God tells us to do.

May we be blessed with a Forgiving Spirit,
And a genuine love for one another.

JESUS IS HERE
(A Song)

I can feel the presence of Jesus,
as He carries me through the day.
I can see His many blessings,
as we travel along the way.

I can feel the love of my Savior,
in good times as well as bad.
And I know He will never leave me;
that is why my heart feels glad.

Jesus is always near, always near.
We need never fear, never fear.
He will never leave or forsake us.
Yes my Lord is here, He is here.

I can feel the Holy Spirit,
as He moves within my life.
He warms my heart and gives me peace,
and lightens my burdens and strife.

I can hear Him when He whispers,
and feel His holy power.
He is my reason for living.
I will serve Him 'til my dying hour.

Jesus is always near, He is near.
We need never fear, never fear.
He will never leave or forsake us.
Yes, my Lord is here, He is here.

WALKING THE WALK

There are many who talk the talk;
Spouting words with the greatest of ease.
But it is walking the walk that matters,
And what God really sees.

Talking the talk is what some folk do
To make themselves look good.
But it is much better to just be silent,
Than to not do what Jesus would.

What God wants is righteous action,
If we never utter a sound.
Talking the talk does not really matter,
If righteous actions do not abound.

I asked God to let my words be
Few, true, kind, and necessary
As I travel this narrow way.
He tells me if I walk the walk,
And not just talk the talk;
I will spend eternity with Him someday.

And so my brothers and sisters,
Let us not just talk the talk.
We must strive to be more like Jesus,
And please Him by walking the walk.

THE CHARTERED COURSE

Jesus is our forerunner,
In this very tedious race.
The enemy is all around us,
Vying for Jesus' place.

There is no place that we can go,
Where Jesus has not already been.
He has charted a sacred course
To free us from a world of sin.

We need only to follow Him.
The way has been made clear.
Jesus is our forerunner,
And He is always near.

So as we run this Christian race;
Let us cling to our saving source.
Yes, Jesus is our forerunner;
And His life is the Chartered Course.

May we walk in the path of righteousness all the days of our lives.

OUR TRUSTWORTHY KING

Who, but you Lord,
Can we trust and never doubt?
Who, but you Lord,
Can lift us up and bring us out?

Nobody but you Lord,
Are always there when we call.
Nobody but you Lord,
Can catch us when we fall.

Who, but you Lord,
Has the greatest love for us?
Who, but you Lord,
In whom we can put our trust?

Nobody but you Lord,
Can ease our troubled hearts.
Nobody but you Lord,
Can shower us with sweet rewards.

You, Father, Are Our Trustworthy King!!

LIMITLESS HE IS

There are no limits to what God can do.
He is all powerful,
And His promises are true.

If we but trust Him, and obey His Holy will,
He is ready and waiting,
His promises to fulfill.

Yes, God is waiting just to hear from us.
He showers us with blessings,
When we give Him our trust.

God loves to bless us, it gives Him great joy.
And when we obey Him,
His blessings he will employ.

There are no boundaries, no hills He cannot climb.
His wonders never cease;
Our God is sublime.
YES, LIMITLESS HE IS!

VICTORY

When we say we have the victory,
Do we know what it really means?
Do we take the time to realize
The depth of the words we sing?

I am sure Satan felt victorious
In the Garden of Eden that day.
And again when Jesus died on Calvary,
Satan felt he'd had his way.

But death was swallowed up in victory,
When Jesus rose from the dead.
The sting of death is gone forever,
By the blood that Jesus shed.

I look forward, with great anticipation,
To the day when the trumpet sounds.
The grave will have lost it's victory
When we rise to receive our crowns.

So let us stand fast and remain unmovable
In our service to the Lord.
We have the victory and Satan is defeated,
As we stand in one accord.

HE IS ALWAYS NEAR

The desire to be in God's presence,
Burns deep in my very soul.
His brilliance, power, and majesty
Are too wonderful to behold.

So he sent His precious son Jesus
For the mortal world to see
His brilliance and His glory,
And His love for you and me.

Our Father, His son Jesus, and Holy Spirit,
Are all one and the same.
The enemy is defeated
With just the mentioning of His name.

We thank God for His goodness,
And praise Him relentlessly;
For sending His son to save us
From the destruction of the enemy.

Although we cannot see Him,
We know He is always near.
His Holy Spirit lives inside us,
And erases all doubt and fear.

Be comforted in knowing that God is always near.

FLESH VS. SPIRIT

God knows all about us,
And our struggles from day to day.
He sent His Holy Spirit
To strengthen, and show us the way.

Although our flesh is weak,
God's love will make us strong.
And if we but only ask Him,
He will keep us from all wrong.

Pleasing God is what I long for;
To obey Him and to do His will.
So when I'm faced with temptations,
He will strengthen me not to yield.

So in this daily struggle
Between the flesh and the spirit;
I run to God for shelter,
And he tells me not to fear it.

Because He never leaves me,
And the battle is already won.
He reminds me of the reason
That He sent His precious son.

And when my flesh is weak,
By His power, my spirit soars.
He keeps me from all evil,
And helps me to sin no more.

My God is so wonderful.
His compassion never ceases.

My purpose is to serve Him;
And my flesh He will defeat.

May God strengthen us in our daily struggle against the enemy.

ALL IS WELL

In every trial there is a blessing;
If we trust God, then we can see.
In every storm there is a message,
Of His deepest love for you and me.

No matter what the circumstances,
God's goodness we can feel.
No matter what the enemy does,
Our souls, he cannot steal.

God said He will never leave us,
And His promises are always true.
With God we are victorious,
No matter what Satan tries to do.

If we but look around us,
And take notice of what God has done;
The enemy can never harm us,
Because of the blood of God's precious son.

Yes, All Is Well.

PRECIOUS MOMENTS

Our days here on earth are surely numbered,
And our time is running out.
Why waste one precious moment
With worries, fears, and doubts?

God said He would never leave us,
And He would wipe away our tears.
Why waste one precious moment
Allowing the enemy to create such fears?

We must be forever mindful
That God is in full control.
Why waste one precious moment
With worries and frets about things untold?

Satan is a liar;
And the battle is already won.
Why waste one precious moment
Doubting the victory of God's precious Son?

Three score and ten is all that is promised,
And then we will soon be gone.
Why waste one precious moment?
We must look to our eternal home.

May God strengthen us in faith and trust ,
so as not to waste one precious moment of His gift of life.

A BRAND NEW ME

When I think of where God has brought me from,
my heart just leaps for joy.
He loved me and waited patiently for me
to come to Him, so His grace He could employ.

When I was sinking deep in sin,
He continued to watch over me.
He never left me to stand alone,
because He knew He would set me free.

When He came into my heart,
He renewed my mind and turned my life around.
I thank Him for His grace and mercy,
for I was lost, but now I am found.

The old me has passed away,
and my spirit has been set free.
Jesus came into my life and touched my very soul;
And created A BRAND NEW ME.

My God continue to strengthen us to forsake the flesh,
and live for Him in the spirit.

THE SON

Jesus, the only begotten son of God.
Emmanuel is also His Name.

Sent from Heaven by His Father.
Undaunted is the way that He came.

Son of the living God, our King.
Christmas marks the time that He came.
Heir to the throne, and Prince of Peace,
Righteousness is His claim to fame.
Intercessor for you and me.

Son of God, and our Lord and Savior.
The way, the truth, and the light is He.

So let us celebrate The Son,
And all that He has done;
And all that He has planned for us;
We thank our Lord and Savior, Jesus.

HE COMFORTS ME
(A daughter's testimony)

Though my heart has been heavy,
And my feelings crushed
By some things you have said and done;
There has never been a moment that I have failed
To thank God for His precious son.

For He comforts me

You are dear to me mother, and I want you to know
That my love will never change.
I am growing in God's grace,,
And my life has been rearranged.

For He comforts me

A pure and forgiving heart,
Is the blessing for which I ask,
And God has heard my cry.
I can truly forgive in spite of the pain,
And He is the reason why.

For He comforts me

I thank God for you dear mother,
And my love is true in spite of the pain.
It is by our Father's grace that I can forgive,
And my love will remain the same.

For He comforts me

You will remain in my prayers and forever in my heart;
And on that you can depend.
I will love and respect you dear mother,
Until this life comes to an end.

For He comforts me

AMEN

GOD'S GRACE

To rise above the trials
And tribulations in this place;

To hold on in times of troubles,
And run this tedious race;

To stand before the Master,
As Jesus pleads our case;

To live with Him in paradise,
Is only by God's grace.

NO REGRETS

We need not fret over past mistakes,
And ungodly things we have done.
It was for that very reason
That God sent His precious son.

We need only to confess our sins.
God is faithful and just to forgive.
And with the coming of each new day;
For Him, we can choose to live.

We've been redeemed by the blood of the Lamb.
Our sins have been washed away.
God's mercy shines all around us,
As He grants us another day.

So don't look back my brothers and sisters.
Have no regrets over things of the past.
Be thankful for God's grace and mercy,
And His love that will always last.

A new day has dawned.
Another chance to serve our God.

ATTITUDE OF GRATITUDE

God has done so much for us;
How can we not concede
That we can do nothing all by ourselves,
And this truth we must all believe.

He woke us up this morning,
And started us on our way.
He allowed us to enter His presence
To worship Him again today.

How could we not be thankful,
And give Him honor and praise?
He watches over us, and protects us,
And helps us in so many ways.

An attitude of gratitude
Would make our Savior smile.
He loves it when we worship Him,
Even when life put us on trial.

So bless the Lord at all times.
Let his praises be continuously in your mouth.
Because worshiping Him with thanksgiving,
Is what life is all about.

YOU ARE A CHILD OF GOD

Do you ever stop and wonder,
Just why you are here?
God created you for His pleasure;
That is why He holds you dear.

Do you ever ask the question,
Why you experience so much pain?
Then when you feel you're at your lowest point,
God shelters you from the rain.

Have you ever abandoned;
As if God just didn't understand?
You must be forever mindful,
That you're always in His capable hands.

Do you ever feel you are alone,
In a world where no one seems to care?
It is then that you must look to Jesus;
He will deliver you from despair.

You are richer than you know;
With a love that is from His heart.
You are wonderfully and uniquely made;
You are a child of God.

WE FALL DOWN

Just saying we are sorry,
Is just not enough.
Confession without repentance,
Make liars out of us.

God wants our hearts,
Our souls, and our minds.
He will not just settle
For idle words that are not genuine.

God is faithful to forgive,
And embrace us when we fall;
But we must turn from our sins,
And commit to giving Him our all.

God knows our every thought,
And sees our every deed.
And still He loves us with compassion,
And supplies our every need.

So when we fall down,
We must not despair.
We must look ever to Jesus;
We will always find Him there.

God has promised to never leave nor forsake us.
Hebrews: 13:5

JESUS IS

Have you ever stopped and wondered,
Just who Jesus is?
The Lamb of God, so pure and gentle;
But with power to erase all fears.

The only begotten Son of God,
Is His claim to fame.
No sweeter sound could there ever be,
Than the mentioning of His name.

The Light of the world, and the Prince of Peace;
He so cares for you and me;
That He sacrificed His unblemished life,
And died on Calvary.

My Comforter, Protector, and my Friend;
He means the world to me.
And if you truly want to know who Jesus is;
Read and be blessed by Psalm 103.

MY SAVIOR, MY FRIEND

There is a man named Jesus,
On whom I know I can depend.
His love for me is endless,
He is my Savior and my friend.

He walks with me, and carries me
When I am too weak to stand.
He is always there when I'm in need.
He is my Savior and my friend.

Though the road is sometimes rough,
And trials seem they will never end,
I can call on the name of Jesus;
He is my Savior and my friend.

So when you are down and can't find your way,
There is One I highly recommend.
His name is Jesus, the Son of the Living God.
He is my Savior and my friend.

TOMORROW

I'll not worry about tomorrow;
It will take care of itself.
I will live for God today,
With praise and thanks for all His help.

Today is a wonderful blessing;
And tomorrow may never come.
I will enjoy the beauty of this day,
And give thanks to the Holy One.

God's mercies are everlasting;
And His wonders will never change.
I will thank Him for this day,
And worry not for anything.

Thank you Father for this day.
I will give it back to You;
With worship, praise and thanksgiving
In all that I say and do.

Help me to be forever mindful
That You will take away my sorrow.
Let me live for You today;
And not worry about tomorrow.

SURRENDER ALL

Help us Father God, to surrender all to you.
Help us to seek your will in everything we do.
Let our worship be real, and our hearts remain true.
Yes, help us Lord to surrender all to you.

Bless us Lord, and keep us in your care.
Let our words be kind, and our deeds always fair.
Let us walk righteously with you and never despair.
Please bless us dear Lord, and keep us in your care.

Teach us your will Father, and help us obey.
Help us to serve you more and more each day.
Let us love even our enemies, in your special way.
Yes, teach us your will Lord, and help us obey.

It is your will Lord that must always be done.
Let us not forget the sacrifice of your precious son.
Let us surrender all to you, the Holy one.
Lord, it is your will, not ours, that must be done.

May we not cling to anything of this world,
But surrender all to our Heavenly Father who cares for us.

SIGN SEEKERS

For those of us who are skeptics,
And continue to ask God for signs.
We need only to look around us,
And stop living as if we were blind.

When we opened our eyes this morning,
It was a sign that God was near.
The miracle of our existence,
Is a sign that He is still here.

Stand still and look around
At all the things that God has done.
We need not seek any further signs
Of the existence of the Holy One.

Walking by faith and not by sight,
Is what God wants us to do.
He sent His precious son to save us.
No better proof that His love is true.

May you be strengthened in faith and trust that God is real.

THE TONGUE

The smallest member,
But oh so strong;
It can destroy a nation,
And cause mountains of harm.

Gossip and rumors
Are like the sweetest desert;
Hard to resist,
But can cause so much hurt.

When tempted to speak,
We must not ever forget,
Our words are powerful,
And can cause much regret.

May our words be few,
True, necessary and kind.
Let us die daily to self,
And let the Holy Spirit shine.

There is fire in the tongue.
May we extinguish it with kind words.

CHRISTIAN FELLOWSHIP

There is an old saying
Of which I was reminded today.
Words of wisdom and spoken in love,
To lead and guide me in God's Holy way.

"Association brings on assimilation"
Is how that old saying goes.
A message to the wise:
It helps us avoid the influence of our foes.

To fellowship with Christians
Will strengthen us in God's ways;
While association with the enemy
Can surely sadden our days.

Where two or more are gathered
In the precious name of Jesus;
He is in the midst as we sing and pray,
And without a doubt, He hears us.

So let us take close inventory
Of the company that we keep;
And steer clear of the enemy,
Whose goal is to defeat.

May we grow stronger in the Lord,
Through regular Christian Fellowship.

THE FREE GIFT

Jesus came to save us.
There is no greater love.
He suffered, died, and was buried;
Then rose up to Heaven above.

He did not leave us comfortless.
And all His promises are true.
He sent His Holy Spirit
To watch over me and you.

A free gift, is the Holy Spirit,
Which cannot be bought or sold.
We need only to love and trust the Lord
For His wonders to unfold.

May we be increased in faith,
Which opens the doors to our hearts
To receive
The Free Gift of The Holy Spirit

SAYING VS. DOING

What we do, matters so much more
Than merely what we say.
God is glorified by what we do,
And how we live each day.

Others cannot see our faith,
Until it is put into action.
It is what we do, not what we say,
That gives God satisfaction.

Faith without works is dead,
Is what the Bible tells us.
We must not only speak the Word,
But live our lives for Jesus.

To do His will is our purpose;
And is what pleases God the most.
We must give our lives completely,
To the Father, Son, and Holy Ghost.

May Our Words Be Always Reflected In Our Actions.

ALL THE TIME, GOD IS GOOD

There is never a time,
When God is not near;
Not a problem He cannot solve,
Not a prayer He does not hear.

Undeserved blessings,
Are showered upon us each day.
We need only to look up,
And never cease to pray.

In the midst of all adversity,
Satan would have us stray.
Bur our Master is always watching,
And ready to show us the way.

"God is good all the time,"
Is not just a ritualistic phrase.
It is a truth that we can trust,
And depend on all our days.

Yes, God IS good all the time,
And ALL the time He is good.

GOD'S PROPERTY

Psalms 21:1 says:
"The earth is the Lord's,
And the fullness thereof;
The world and they that dwell therein."
Not a single thing belongs to us;
It all belongs to Him.

The food we eat, the clothes we wear,
And even the air we breathe;
Are all on loan to us.
We are but caretakers of His wondrous gifts;
So in Him we must place our trust.

Let us never think too highly of ourselves,
Or look down on one another.
For we too, are nothing within ourselves;
But are a part of our Father's property.

May we rejoice in the abundance of God's giving;
And never forget,
He is the reason for our living.

THE SIMPLE TRUTH

Jesus came to save the world,
And free us from a world of sin.
A truth so simple that it sometimes defies
The understanding if mortal men.

Some folk seek much more complicated truths,
And boast about all the good things they have done;
While ignoring the most simple truth,
That salvation comes only through God's Holy Son.

Some are seekers of power and wealth,
And worldly things that flatter;
And make them look powerful in the eyes of men,
While losing sight of what really matters.

But the key to salvation, my brothers and sisters,
Is not complicated, but simple and true.
Jesus Christ is the Son of God,
And saving us is what He came to do.

If we believe, and have faith in this Simple Truth,
We Are Saved.

THE POINT OF PAIN

When we have troubles and feelings of despair,
We must never forget our Savior is still there.
He never slumbers and He never sleeps;
And all his promises, He is faithful to keep.

When we trust the Lord,
And take Him at His word,
Our every request
Is sure to be heard.

His Holy Spirit teaches us,
And helps us to grow,
Preparing us for that special day
When there will be troubles no more.

God knows us much better
Than we know ourselves.
He limits our suffering
To what He knows we can bear.

So the point of our pain
Is really quite clear.
We gain strength in all adversity
Because our Savior is near.

May the pain of all adversities be eased by God's ever presence.

THE BLOOD

We need not rationalize our sins,
For they are why Jesus came.
We must confess and then repent;
So His blood was not shed in vain.

There is no greater love,
Than what Jesus has for us.
He suffered and died on Calvary,
And His sacrifice, we can trust.

He promised to never leave us,
And on that we can depend.
Although not one is good enough,
His mercies never end.

When Satan tries to steal our joy,
And attacks us like a raging flood;
Jesus lovingly pulls us close and whispers
'You are covered by The Blood'.

GRACEFUL YOUTH

Our youth of Grace Emmanuel
Are a joy to behold.
As they praise and worship Jesus,
We watch their gifts unfold.

There are those who serve as ushers,
An important task it is said.
They keep the gates wide open,
Welcoming worshipers to be fed.

There are those who lift their voices,
And bring sweet music to our ears.
They sound so sweet and gentle,
We can hardly hold back the tears.

There are those who dance, and actors too;
Whose gifts have blessed us so.
As they praise and worship Jesus,
And let their spirits flow.

We thank God for you dear children;
And we love you beyond compare.
You were sent to us from Heaven;
God's gift for us to share.

THE BIG QUESTION
(Are we walking the walk?)

Is what we do in line with what we say?

Do we die to self daily, and let God have His way?

Are we angry and bitter over things of the past?

Are we more concerned about things that will not last?

Have we truly forgiven the transgressions of others?

Do we genuinely love our sisters and brothers?

Are we honoring God with the first fruits of our labor?

Do we look up to Him and trust in His favor?

Are our hearts pure and our words true?

Are we doing each day what God wants us to do?

It is oh so easy to TALK THE TALK.
But God is pleased when we WALK THE WALK.

May God strengthen us to be obedient in our daily walk.

OUR SAVIOR

There is so much adversity
In this world today.
Many trials and tribulations
Are sure to come our way.

We can run to the arms of Jesus
When this world seems too much to bear.
In His arms He will hold us gently,
And will deliver us from despair.

Jesus is our shelter.
He is never far from us.
He shields us from the enemy,
And His promises we can trust.

There are demons all around us,
But we need not fret nor fear.
Jesus is our shelter,
And He is always near.

We Can Trust The Presence And The Power Of
Jesus Always.

NO POWER
(A Song Of Thanksgiving)

Satan you don't have no power here.
Ohhh, Satan you don't have no power here.
I have heard the Master's voice,
And He has made it clear,
That Satan has no power here.

Jesus woke me up this morning and made it clear.
He has spoken to my spirit oh so clear.
He has told me what to do,
And has told me what to say.
So Satan you don't have no power here.

I will praise my Savior all the day.
I will let His Holy Spirit have His way.
I will do the Master's will,
And my heart He will fulfill.
So Satan you don't have no power here.

My God is such an awesome God.
He sustains me and cleanses my heart.
He has touched by very soul,
And His love has made me whole.
So Satan you don't have no power here.

Ohhh Satan you don't have no power here.
Ohhh Satan you don't have no power here.
I have heard the Master's voice,
And He has made it clear.
That Satan has no power here.

OUR FIRST, OUR LAST, OUR EVERYTHING

Jesus wakes us up each morning,
And He carries us through each day.
He watches over us when are sleeping,
And He hears us when we pray.

Not for one moment are we without Him,
He is always standing by.
He rejoices at our laughter,
And wipes our tears when we cry.

When everyone else forsakes us,
There is one on whom we can depend.
Our Lord and Savior Jesus,
Whose love and mercies never end.

So as we juggle our busy schedules,
Let us not neglect our Lord and King.
We must take time to give Him thanks and praise.
He is our First, our Last, our Everything.

II

Bereavement in Rhyme

As surely as we are born, we must die. In spite of this realization, we are often at a lost for words in the consolation of others as they grieve the loss of loved ones. The following are a few of the poems I have shared with friends who I hold dear.

HER JOURNEY HAS JUST BEGUN

Be of good cheer in knowing,
That you loved ones' journey has just begun.
And that they is walking with their savior,
leaning on His everlasting arm.

Listen closely and you can hear them;
There's no sadness in their voice.
They are talking with the Master.
Oh what a time to rejoice!

Listen closer children of God,
There's sweet music in the air.
They are singing with the angels,
Without a worry or a care.

Hush.....stand still and listen,
As they remember us all prayer.
They are humbly asking Jesus,
if one day they can meet us there.

Look up and you can see them,
As bright as the noonday sun.
They are in the arms of Jesus.
Their new lives have just begun.

SANDY

*Our Father in Heaven
Has shown you His love.
He has received your father
Into His kingdom above.*

Thanks Be To God

KEEP THE FAITH

Beautiful flowers have been picked from among us.
Their sweet fragrances will be truly missed.
God wanted them to enhance His garden;
So He called them to their eternal rest.

I can visualize them smiling;
In anticipation of our heavenly home.
They are walking among the angels;
And praising God with the sweetest song.

What a glorious time they must be having;
Meeting and greeting the Saints of old.
Listen closely and you can hear them,
As their prayers for us unfold.

Their faith is as strong as ever;
As yours and mine must be.
We must continue to praise our Master;
And someday we too, shall be free.

May God Bless Us With Unshakable Faith.

MARILYN
(She Still Lives)

*In our hearts and in our minds
She will never die.
She has answered the Master's call,
And we need not question why.*

She Still Lives

*As much as we all love her,
Our heavenly Father loves her more.
So He called her to live forever
On a quiet and peaceful shore.*

She Still Lives

*A more gentle, kind, and loving soul,
There could never be.
Her compassion and concern for others
Was a beautiful sight to see.*

She Still Lives

*Listen closely and you can hear her.
There is no sadness in her voice.
She is walking among the angels.*

Oh what a time to rejoice!

Marilyn Still Lives
May God Keep Us In Perfect Peace Until We See Her Again.

GOING HOME I

The sun has set on a blessed soul.
She has heard the master's voice.
And though she will be missed so very much;
In her going home we can rejoice.

She has entered the gates of heaven,
With a smile upon her face.
For she understands her destiny,
And has received the Master's grace.

If she had the opportunity,
To turn back the hands of time;
She would not question the Master's will,
But would pray for those who are left behind.

Though your hearts are aching dear friends of
mine;
You can hold on, and never fret.
She has gone home to be with Jesus;
And for that, she has no regrets.

May God strengthen you in your acceptance of His will;
And bless you with increased comfort in your time of sorrow.

GOING HOME II

In God's infinite wisdom,
He has called your father home.
And now he joins your beloved mother,
As they kneel before the throne.

Be of good cheer my dear friend ;
Their reunion is sanctioned by God.
They are in the Master's loving care,
Never again to be apart.

As much as you love them both;
Our Heavenly Father loves them more.
So He called them up to Heaven,
To a quiet and peaceful shore.

So let not your heart be troubled,
God is still in full control.
He will surely give you strength
To let His will unfold.

May God Bless You With Unshakable Faith

IN THE ARMS OF JESUS I

The gates of Heaven have opened,
To welcome your precious child.
She has been called to rest in peace,
In a world that is undefiled.

As much as you love your dear one,
Our Heavenly Father loves her more.
God has called her to live forever,
On a quiet and peaceful shore.

Never will she know the troubles
That this cruel world can bring.
She has entered a higher realm,
Where only love and goodness reign.

So may your hearts be filled with gladness;
Because your loved one has been set free.
She is in the arms of Jesus,
And there is no better place to be.

IN THE ARMS OF JESUS II

Your dear brother Ola,
Has answered the Master's voice.
His race has been run, and he is at rest,
And for this, you can rejoice.

He has entered a wonderful place,
Where only goodness and mercy abide.
His Father has embraced him,
And will never leave his side.

No more pain or sorrow
Will your brother ever endure.
He is in the arms of Jesus,
And his destiny is sure.

Listen closely and you can almost hear him.
There's sweet music in the air.
He is singing with the angels,
Without a worry or a care.

May the everlasting arms of Jesus comfort you always.

With Deepest Love & Sympathy

NEW LIFE HAS JUST BEGUN

Be of good cheer in knowing,
That you loved ones' journey has just begun.
And that they is walking with their savior,
leaning on His everlasting arm.

Listen closely and you can hear them;
There's no sadness in their voice.
They are talking with the Master.
Oh what a time to rejoice!

Listen closer children of God,
There's sweet music in the air.
They are singing with the angels,
Without a worry or a care.

Hush.....stand still and listen,
As they remember us all prayer.
They are humbly asking Jesus,
if one day they can meet us there.

Look up and you can see them,
As bright as the noonday sun.
They are in the arms of Jesus.
Their new lives have just begun.

GRACE

God gave us a precious angel
Who brought joy into our lives.
And now He has reclaimed her;
And removed all pain and strife.

Though our time with her was much too short;
Sweet memories shall remain.
For those who knew and love her;
Life will never be the same.

Our lives are better for having known her;
A precious gift from Heaven above.
But God's plan for her takes precedence;
There is no greater love.

Listen closely and you can hear the angels,
As they sing a sweet refrain.
She is in the arms of Jesus;
And waiting to see us again.

So let not your heart be troubled my friend,
She is in the Master's care.
And He will bless and keep us,
Until we meet her there.

May God's loving arms continue to enfold you

HE HEARD THE MASTER'S VOICE

As much as you love him my friend,
His heavenly father loves him more.
So He called him up to heaven,
To a quiet and peaceful shore.

He is in the Master's loving arms;
Not a tear will he ever shed.
His savior is caressing him gently,
And he is no way afraid.

Jesus has smiled on your dear son;
Oh what a time to rejoice.
He is singing with the angels,
Because he heard the Master's voice.

So be of good cheer in knowing
That he is in the Master's care;
And though he will be sadly missed,
God will deliver you from despair.

HE HEARD THE MASTER'S VOICE.

MOMORIES IN THE WIND

It is my hope that this wind chime
will bring sweet memories of her
precious smile and gentle ways.

And when it chimes, may you know
That her presence is near,
to ease your pain and brighten your days.

Know also my friend, that you are the
Epitome of the good son, as well she knew.

And now she is in the Master's care;
So you need not worry for His promises are true.

He is surrounding her with beauty unseen,
and keeping her in His loving care.

What a glorious day it will be,
when we arrive and meet her there.

So be not dismayed, my precious friend.
Sweet memories will sustain you
as this chime blows in the wind.

MEMORIES OF AN ANGEL

It is my hope that this plant
Will bring sweet memories of your
Mother's precious smile and gentle ways.

And as it flourishes,
May you know that her presence is near,
To ease your pain and brighten your days.

Know too, my friend,
That you are not alone,
As you grieve your mother's passing.
But be of good cheer in knowing,
That her future is everlasting.

She has heard the Master's call;
And has gladly answered His voice.
She has entered His heavenly kingdom;
And for that we can rejoice.

Let not your heart be troubled.
It is said that life is only a test;
A test which your mother has passed;
And been rewarded with peace and sweet rest.

HIS SPIRIT LIVES

Life will never be the same
For anyone who knew him.
His kindness touched so many lives,
And so many of us loved him.

A more giving person you will never meet.
Frank's heart was big and true.
He had so much love for everyone,
And loving him was so easy to do.

God blessed him with a loving spirit;
A kind heart and the gift of giving.
The world was surely a better place,
By his caring and his style of living.

So be of good cheer in knowing
That this is only the beginning.
And that one day we will meet again,
with joy that is never ending.

NEVER ALONE I

It grieves me dear Doris,
that I have been unaware.
Had I known you lost you grandmother,
I would certainly have been there.

Please know that you are never alone;
and you always have a friend.
Our Lord and Savior, Jesus Christ,
whose compassion never ends.

God Loves You, And So Do I.

YOU ARE NEVER ALONE II

In our Savior's infinite wisdom,
He has called your loved one home.
But do not despair my dear friend,
You are never alone.

What a blessing it is to know the Lord,
And to trust His Holy will.
To know that in your darkest hour,
His promises, He will fulfill.

God said He will never leave us,
And His promises are true.
So look up, stand fast, and trust Him.
He will take care of you.

You are our sister and our friend,
And we share your time of grief.
Please know that you are never alone,
And in God there is sweet relief.

May you be comforted by the power of the Holy Spirit.

I WEEP
(With Tears Of Joy)

When I think of God's goodness,
And all He has done for me;
I sing His praises and worship Him,
But I cannot help but weep.

To think of God's only begotten Son,
Who had the power to avoid the cross;
But He suffered, died, and was buried,
So that our souls would not be lost.

Oh what an awesome God we serve.
His mercies never cease.
He sent His Son to pay our debts;
And the enemy to defeat.

Yes, when I think of His goodness,
I cannot help bet weep;
With tears of sorrow, but more of joy,
That our Savior no longer sleeps.

May Our Weeping Be of Joy That He Lives

THE LONG ROAD HOME

No one promised it would be easy;
Life's road with it's crooks and turns.
It's hills and valleys will surely come,
And are as sure as the morning sun.

We sometimes wonder if we will survive,
With troubles and heartaches by the ton.
But when we listen, we can hear the voice of Jesus
Saying the battle is already won.

He assures us of His presence,
And tells us just what to do.
No matter what the enemy does,
Jesus will always see us through.

So though the road is sometimes rough,
And our burdens seem hard to bear;
We need but to look to Jesus,
And trust that He is near.

He will comfort us in our sorrows,
And ease our troubled minds.
And though He may not remove the mountains,
He will give us the strength to climb.

The long road home is easier traveled when we put
our trust in Jesus.

PRESENT WITH THE LORD

Though your hearts are filled with sorrow,
And you are feeling so much pain;
Know that God is always faithful.
He will comfort and sustain.

She is in the arms of Jesus,
Without a worry or a care.
He has picked a precious flower.
No more burdens will she bear.

As much as you love her dear Betty and family,
Her Heavenly Father loves her more.
He has called her to be with Him,
On a quiet and peaceful shore.

So look up and feel God's presence.
We are all on one accord.
To be absent from our bodies,
Is to be present with the Lord.

May the grace of God sustain you in your sorrow.

TO TOM WITH LOVE

I will miss your smile,
And your gentle ways;
The conversations we shared,
That brightened my days.

Your soft spoken ways,
And friendliness to all,
Made you very special,
As all who knew you can easily recall.

There were times when I felt
Everything was going wrong.
Your words of encouragement
Gave me a happier song.

Yes I will miss you Tom,
As so many others will.
But I know in my heart,
Your spirit is with us still.

I asked God to remember you with His kindness,
And He heard my prayer.
He called you to be with Him,
And there is no better place than there.

God loves you Tom, and so do I

III

Love in Rhyme

*"Love is joy, love is pain, love is laughter in the rain;"
such a truthful lyric from the voice of Natalie Cole in her
song "I've Got Love On My Mind." The following
poems were inspired by the joys and perils of love; some
upon the request of friends, and others from my own
experiences.*

THE STRUGGLE TO LOVE

As mere human beings, we struggle to love
Those who persecute and lie on us.
It is then that we must call on our powerful God
To strengthen, keep us, and increase our trust.

It is easy, and without reward
To love those who love us.
The struggle is in loving our enemies
As God says we must.

To do this alone,
Is an impossible task for us.
We must lean not to our own understanding,
But seek God first.

He will strengthen us to love
Even those who persecute and lie on us.
So we need not be discouraged;
Just keep the faith, love, and trust.

ARIANNA
You Are:

Sunshine on rainy days.
A twinkling star on which to gaze.

A full and beautiful moon.
A lovely flower in full bloom.
A summer breeze to cool my soul.

A delightful breath of Spring.
Ari, you are all these things.

AND MORE!!

I LOVE YOU!!

HAPPY 8TH BIRTHDAY

Grand MaMa

ROBBIE III

God blessed us Robbie,
The day you were born.
Our hearts were filled with joy.
We were all expecting a little girl,
But God said it would be a boy.

You were a wonderful surprise,
And you brought joy into my heart.
You will always be as special to me,
As you have been from the very start.

May your steps be ordered by the Master;
And you grow in His grace all the days of your life.

I Love You
Grand Ma Ma

WE THANK GOD FOR YOU

An inspiration to us all,
You make God's messages so clear.
And deliver them with such sweet passion,
For all Christian ears to hear.

You are empowered by the Holy Spirit
With faith that is plain to see.
A true servant of the Master;
No greater Pastor could there be.

We marvel at your energy
When you are excited by the Word.
The messages you give, and the songs you sing
Are the sweetest we have ever heard.

So know Pastor, how much you are appreciated,
And how very much you are loved.
For us, you are a very special gift,
Sent directly from Heaven above.

Pastor Jennings, We Thank God For You.

A TIME FOR REST

An anointed man of God you are;
Unselfish in all your ways.
You bring joy into so many lives,
And brighten so many days.

An inspiration to the young,
And a blessing to the old;
It is through your love and dedication,
That so many blessings unfold.

You are a blessing to so many,
And you always do your best.
But now it is time my dear friend Quinton,
For you to get some rest.

I will keep you in my prayers,
And hope you hear this plea.
Relax and take some time for self.
My prayer is that God will strengthen thee.

BLESSED EVENT

You are anxiously awaiting
A most blessed event.
The angel you are expecting
Is surely Heaven sent.

May your days be filled with happiness,
And sprinkled with mounds of joy;
As you grow oh so much closer
To the welcoming of your baby boy.

Oops! I'm sorry Indira,
I guess my head was in a whirl.
An Angel just reminded me
That you're having baby girl.

Congratulations!!!

YOUR SPECIAL DAY

We were blessed beyond measure
The day that you were born.
God knew our paths would surely cross,
And great friendships would be formed.

A very special lady you are;
And a true blue friend indeed.
The world would surely be a better place
If more people would follow your lead.

You are thoughtful and kind to all people you meet;
And can bring a smile to the saddest face.
Yours is a special kind of love
That's why God keeps you in His grace.

I thank God for you dear Dee.
You can brighten the darkest day,
With your cheerful "what's up good looking;"
It's magical....what can I say?

EVERLASTING LOVE I

*May you always be as happy
as you are today;
And God continue to bless you
in a very special way.*

*May the love you share grow stronger,
and last forever;
and your friendship flourish,
as you journey through life together.*

*Let your ways be gentle,
and your words be kind;
with mutual respect
to insure peace of mind.*

*Groom, demonstrate your love for your bride
in everything you do and say;
and never allow pride stand in your way.*

*Bride, receive your groom's love,
and return it with all your heart;
so that nothing and no one can ever tear you apart.*

*Bride and Groom,
This is the first day of the rest of your lives.
May you forever be as much in love as you are today.
And may God bless you in a very special way.*

EVERLASTING LOVE II

God has blessed your union.
It has withstood the test of time.
Fifty years of wedded bliss,
and a true love that is sublime.

Groom, you are very blessed
to have a wonderful woman in your life.
God, in His infinite wisdom,
chose her to be your wife.

And Bride, you are also blessed
that your husband was led to you.
One who is obedient to God's will,
and showers you with love so true.

So may the next fifty years bring
enormous blessings to you from Heaven above.
And may your union grow even stronger.
For yours is truly an Everlasting Love.

WEDDED BLISS

God has blessed you with a lovely bride,
To walk humbly by your side.
Someone to share your hopes and dreams,
And keep your spirits alive.

Give her love and respect throughout your days,
And your marriage will be blessed.
Keep her close in all your ways,
And God will do the rest.

Show her kindness and never fail
To tell her of your love so true.
Treat her gently and cherish her,
And she will give it back to you.

May God bless your union with JOY
And HAPPINESS throughout your years.

FRIENDS FOREVER

When I think of you my friend,
As I so often do;
I am very thankful
To have a friend like you.

God places people in our lives
For very specific reasons.
Some friendships are but for a little while,
But ours is for all seasons.

Thoughts of you always bring a smile,
And warm feelings to my heart.
I appreciate your friendship.
It has been a blessing from the very start.

So know, my friend, you are in my prayers
Each and every day.
Our friendship means so much to me;
Even more than words can say.

May God Bless Us With An Everlasting Friendship

KEEP THE FAITH

The eyes of the Lord
are upon you my dear Celeste.
And His ears are open
to your cry.

May you be blessed
with the deepest faith,
and keep your eyes toward the sky.

May His Healing Power Embrace You Always

GOD'S SAVING GRACE

It was a spiritual revelation
That brought us to this place.
I was physically, emotionally, and spiritually
downtrodden
When God blessed me with His Grace.

He spoke to me so clearly;
Even calling out our Pastor's name.
And since we have committed to His will,
Our lives have never been the same.

God led us to this place of worship,
Where so much love abides.
My family could see the change in me,
And they rallied by my side.

Our very precious daughter ,
Has been showered with so much love.
Her excitement around the children's choir
Is a gift from Heaven above.

When we look back over the years,
At how truly blessed we are;
We thank God for His Saving Grace;
And His giving us a brand new start.

OUR JOY

We look forward to your coming,
Our little "Bundle Of Joy."
And it really does not matter
If you are a girl or a boy.

You are so very special;
A gift from heaven above.
We can hardly wait to hold you,
And shower you with love.

The beginning of a blessed journey,
Is what your birthday will bring.
Your day will always be special;
A cause for our hearts to sing.

We thank God for a precious angel;
A blessing He did employ.
Our hearts are filled with gladness,
In anticipation of Our Joy.

FAMILY
(Celebration of Reunion)

We are family,
Surrounded by so much love.
Each one, a gift to the other;
A blessing from Heaven above.

I thank God for each of you;
The young as well as the old.
You are each a very special gift,
And wonderful to behold.

Coming together in Christian love
Has truly warmed my heart;
And reminds me of just how much I am blessed,
Knowing that nothing can keep us apart.

God has blessed us with this gathering,
And the celebration of our life together.
Let us be forever mindful of His goodness,
And praise His Holy name forever.

May God continue to hold our family together in
Christian love,
until we celebrate the ultimate reunion in His
Kingdom for all eternity.

TRUE BLUE FRIEND

A true friend in need is what you are;
And I thank God for you.
You've been there for me when times were hard,
With a love that is genuine and true.

I will never forget your kindness
And support when I needed it most.
You sacrificed, and was there for me,
Even when your own spirits were low.

When others stand back and wish me well;
It's you who step up to the plate,
With words of wisdom and a genuine love
That inspires me to run my race.

Yes, a true friend in need is what you are,
And I do thank God for you.
May He keep you in His loving care,
And bless you in all you do.

130

THE SECOND PEW

It was in the second pew,
During a church service that we met.
From the very beginning it was plain to see
That your destiny, and mine were set.

We were destined to become good friends;
Joined together for a special reason.
To be supportive of each other,
And not just for a season.

How ironic that we are both Southern girls,
From towns just a few miles apart.
Even attended the same school of higher learning;
We were destined to meet from the very start.

And then, we migrated North;
Never knowing our time to meet would soon be due.
After several years of missing each other,
We ended up in the second pew.

Now as we sing and praise the Lord;
That pew is second nature.
And we thank our Heavenly Father
For our friendship both now and in the future.

May God continue to bless us with a friendship that is true.
And may it be strengthened as we praise Him in the Second Pew.

(To Thelma with love)

A MOTHER'S LOVE

Through all the heartaches,
And all the pain,
A mother's love remains the same.

Unconditional and without question,
Her love is strong and true.
No matter how rough the road,
She always sees it through.

Her tasks are many and sometimes tough;
They span through many years'
But still she holds her head up high,
And smiles right through the tears.

She is always there in a time of need
To lend a helping hand.
And although her heart is often aching,
She does the best she can.

No one can take a mother's place;
God's special gift to all mankind.
Her love can brighten the darkest day;
Like a ray of bright sunshine.

Thank God for a mother's love,
On which we can always depend.
May God keep our mothers in His loving care,
Until the end of the world....Amen.

132

FAITHFUL SERVANT

Your name is synonymous with caring,
And it shows in all you do.
You are truly a faithful servant,
And we are thankful for you.

Your concern and compassion for children
Are very special gifts from God.
He smiles as you give so much of yourself,
While humbly seeking no rewards.

Barbara Griffith Wilson
You are a true and giving soul,
With a genuine quest for service,
And a heart as pure as gold.

We thank you Barbara, for all you do.
You are loved by us, one and all.
You are truly a blessing from Heaven.
We thank God for your answering His call.

May God continue to Bless You In Your Service To People

HAPPY BIRTHDAY ROBBIE
(My Son)

God blessed me with an angel
The day He gave me you.
A good son is what you truly are;
And I thank God for you.

You have made me proud through all your years,
And have never caused me pain.
You brought so much joy into my life,
And today it is still the same.

When I count my blessings my darling son,
You are at the very top
I thank God for blessing me with
The very cream of the crop.

So celebrate your special day,
And know that you are loved.
Mere words could never say how much;
Because you were sent from up above.

I love you eternally
Ma

A VERY SPECIAL MOM

Although I may not tell you often,
How much you mean to me;
You are very, very special,
And you will always be.

I sometimes take for granted,
Just how wonderful you really are.
But there could never be a better mother,
If I searched both near and far.

I thank you Mom, for all the love you've shown,
And all the things you've done.
If I could choose from a million Moms,
You would certainly be the one.

Yes, you are very special Mom,
And I love you with all my heart.
I thank God that you are my mother,
And nothing can ever tear us apart.

MY BELOVED WIFE

God smiled on me from Heaven,
The day he gave me you.
No greater gift could He have given,
Than our love so genuine and true.

And when I count my blessings,
As I so often do;
Your gentle smile and lovely ways
Always come shining through.

I have not said thank you nearly enough,
For all you have done for me.
You have been my love, and my closest friend;
As you will forever be.

No flower compares to your beauty;
It out shines the brightest star.
I thank God for you my dearest;
And I love you with all my heart.

INCREDIBLE LOVE

When I think about the love of God,
It thrills me through and through.
Just knowing how much He cares for me,
And that His promises to us are true.

He promised to never leave us,
And on that we can depend.
He assures us throughout His word,
That He will always be our friend.

John 3:16 is very clear
About God's love, excluding none.
It says He so loved the world
That He gave His only begotten son.

What greater love could there ever be,
Than what God has for us?
He suffered and died on the cross,
And in Him we must place our trust.

Oh what an incredible love
God has for you and me!
Let us praise Him to the utmost,
Until his blessed face we see.

TO RITA WITH LOVE

You are such a faithful servant,
And I am so inspired by you.
Your love and dedication to the Lord
Is a beacon that comes shinning through.

You were the first to pray for me
When God led me to this place.
Your warmth and kindness on that day
Can never be erased.

When I count my blessings Rita,
I can certainly speak of you.
I thank God for your teachings,
And your faith so strong and true.

May God keep you in his loving care,
And strengthen you to do His will.
It's through kind and gentle servants like you
That His promises are fulfilled.

Thank you Rita, for your dedication to my Sunday school class.

HAPPY BIRTHDAY SIS

Today is your birthday sis,
And one thing is very true.
No other sister in all the world
Could be as kind as you.

You have a loving spirit
That is giving, true, and kind.
When God granted me a sister,
I am thankful that He made you mind.

I almost cried when I heard you say
You didn't expect to live to sixty two.
I thank God that you are here today,
Because I love and cherish you.

So enjoy this, your special day dear sis;
And I wish you all the best.
You are loved much more than words can say.
And as a sister, you're worlds above the rest.

HAPPY BIRTHDAY
TO MY OTHER MOTHER

God smiled on me
When He gave me you.
He blessed with another mother,
So kind and so true.

Through all the years
You have shown such strength;
A true model of courage
And of love and contentment.

Your presence in my life
Has meant so much to me.
The warmth of your smile
Is such a joy to see.

I thank God for you Mama Rushia,
On this, your special day.
May He keep you in His loving care,
And bless you in a special way.

GOD IS IN IT
(A tribute to Pastor David Clark)

You came before us and preached God's word
With such clarity that it touched my soul.
God's presence was so very clear,
And His majesty did unfold.

He used you in a mighty way,
And blessed all who heard your voice.
I thank God for your anointing;
Another blessing for which to rejoice.

I pray that you will never tire,
Of sharing your gift of love.
You're a beacon of hope, a man of God,
A special gift from Heaven above.

So may God bless you Rev. Clark,
And keep you in His loving care.
It is because of anointed saints like you,
That God's flock will not despair.

God is truly in it!!

GOD'S GIFT

Alicia, you are truly God's creation,
With a smile that warms the heart.
A gracious lady is what you are;
A gift to me from God.

From the very first time we met,
I could feel a glow of love.
The kind of glow that only comes
From our savior up above.

You are such an inspiration to me;
A friend that I do treasure.
I wish you love, joy, and peace,
And blessings beyond measure.

On this your special day my friend;
May the love of God enfold you.
May you realize the desires of your heart,
And your every wish come true.

HAPPY BIRTHDAY
God's Gift

Children are very special.
They are God's gift from up above.
He is blessing you with a little one,
As a reflection of His love.

May God keep you in His loving care,
And bless your baby too;
To know that God is all we need,
And that His love is true.

May God keep you and yours in His loving care.

A SPECIAL GIFT

You have been an inspiration to many;
And served others for so many years.
You have helped to mold so many lives,
And dried so many tears.

Because you cared, lives have been changed
For people who were in despair.
Broken families have been renewed
By the knowledge that you have shared.

Your dedication to helping others
Has been a wonder to behold.
And for many, your Hog Trough Theory
Is among the greatest stories ever told.

You are truly a special gift Mr. Keaton;
With services tried and true.
Your contributions will always be cherished,
And I thank God for you.

HAPPY 87TH BIRTHDAY

QUEEN

This day is very special.
It's the day that you were born.
God smiled upon your mother,
And gave you to her.
Then He rapped His arms around you,
Nurtured you, and made you His very own.

But He shared His precious gift
With those of us who know you.
And we all too, fell in love.

You are a wonderful daughter,
Wife, mother, and friend Pepper;
And I thank God for your friendship.
And although our schedules hinder our fellowship;
You are always in my heart.

Our friendship is very special.
It is fertilized with a genuine love
That doesn't fade in the distance.
And I do thank God for you dear friend.

May God bless you immeasurably;
This day, and every day to come.

Happy Birthday Queen

SISTERS

You are my oldest sister,
And I look up to you.
You are a very trusting soul,
And my love for you is true.

I may not always tell you
Just how much you mean to me;
But know that you are loved dear June,
As well you will always be.

God Loves You And So Do I

MAJESTIC LADY
(On Your Retirement)

Today, dear lady, we celebrate your retirement,
And your move to a higher plane
Of relaxation, shopping, and just being free,
And the joys that retirement will bring.

The years have served you well,
With blessings of grace and beauty.
You served impeccably in the workplace,
Never failing to do your duty.

So tall and statuesque you are;
A beauty to behold.
Always with a cheerful smile,
You are a gracious soul.

And not just your outer beauty;
Your spirit glows as well.
A loving wife, mother, and friend;
As all who know you can tell.

So go forth "Tall Ann,"
With the world as your stage and resource.
And my God keep you in His loving care,
As you chart your retirement course.

CONGRATULATIONS MAJESTIC LADY!

147

IT IS WELL

I prayed for you this morning dear pastor;
And I know God heard my prayer.
He has sent a guardian angel,
To keep you in His care.

You are loved and truly missed;
And your absence leaves such a void.
We look forward to your healing,
By the grace of our saving Lord.

May His arms embrace your body,
And heal you from head to toe.
May His grace and mercy enfold you;
And His blessings never cease to flow.

I will keep you in my prayers dear pastor;
And trust in God's healing power,
To keep you in His loving care,
And strengthen you by the hour.

IT IS WELL

MELANCHOLY MOMENTS

Not in a negative sense,
Do I dream of you my dear.
The memory of your smile,
Just makes me want you near.

As I listen to my favorite song,
Luther sounds so much like you.
The words warm my heart,
And reaffirms my love so true.

So buy me a rose,
If only imaginary.
The thought is just as real.
And cheers me momentarily.

My heart is open to you always,
And melancholy moments will soon fade away.
But the love I have for you,
Grows stronger day by day.

MY ETERNAL FRIEND

Deborah

May you rise above every adversity,
Defeat every enemy,
Excel in every task,
Weather every storm,
And walk in the path of righteousness,
With God's smile illuminating
Your path always.
I Thank God for putting you in my life

I love you

LOOK UP SISTER

Sister girl, you have been on my mind,
And in my heart each time I kneel to pray.
I have asked the Lord to lift you up,
And guide you along your way.

Though times may be hard and the road oh so rough;
God has never left your side.
He is patiently waiting to hear from you;
So that your needs He can provide.

He says in His word that he will never leave you;
And on that you can depend.
He is not only your loving Savior;
But He wants to be your friend.

Open the door to your heart sister girl,
And let the Master in.
He will lift you up and dry your tears,
And deliver you from a world of sin.

So look up sister, and behold His Majesty.
Let Him mend your broken heart.
He looks forward to your coming to Him.
He's been with you from the very start.

MIGHTY MEN OF GOD

Grace Emmanuel, we are so very blessed
To have such mighty men of God.
They gracefully praise and serve the Lord
With dedication that warms the heart.

Jesus said, "Go ye into all the world,
And preach the gospel to every creature."
The mighty men of Grace Emmanuel
Are proclaiming Jesus as their teacher.

Such mighty men of grace you are,
Who stand humbly before our Lord,
Proclaiming the gospel of Jesus Christ,
As you serve in sweet accord.

Men of grace is who you are,
And praising God is what you do.
Mighty men of Grace Emmanuel,
We are so very proud of you.

MISSING YOU ALREADY

Yours is a smile that brightens everyone's day,
And brings joy to saddened hearts.
I'm missing you even before you go,
And dreading that we must part.

You're such a nice person Kellie;
So genuine and so real.
I've enjoyed so much working with you;
Words can't express how sad I feel.

Working with you is such a joy,
And parting brings so much sorrow.
But my prayers are with you wherever you go.
God's speed dear Kellie today and for all tomorrows.

MY DOCTOR, MY FRIEND
(mother & her physician)

So many times you have treated me
With the greatest of medical care.
No words can express my gratitude
For your always being there.

My fears were calmed by your gentle smile,
And genuine concern for me.
And when it comes to competence ,
No greater physician could there ever be.

With God as your guide, you've been a blessing
To every patient you have seen.
But a special blessing from heaven above
Is what you have been to me.

So as you retire Dr. Gordon,
Please remember that this is true;
There will never be another doctor
As loved and appreciated as you.

A Caring Physician
(Dr. Scott Taylor)

When I think of your intervention
With a suicidal child;
It warms my heart and gives me joy,
And even makes me smile.

You told him you would pray for him,
And you gave him a gentle touch.
I knew that God was present,
And your kindness meant so much.

You are not just a physician;
But God's child, it was plain to see.
The love you showed toward that young man,
Might well have set him free.

I thank God for a caring physician like you,
Who shows love and deep concern.
You are one in a million Dr. Taylor.
May God bless you in return.

TO MY MOTHER, ON MY WEDDING DAY

You, dear Mother, are the reason I am here,
On this my wedding day.
And I love and cherish you
Much more than words can say.

Through all the years you've been there for me
With your kind and gentle touch.
The love you gave, and sacrifices you made;
You have given me oh so much.

Today is a very special day;
One that I hold dear.
And you, my loving Mother,
Are the reason I am here.

Thank you Mother, for all you have done;
And for your sweet and tender ways.
Your special place within my heart
Will remain throughout my days.

CONGRATULATIONS

To An Anointed Servant Of God
Assistant Pastor George Wilkerson

My heart leaped with anticipation
of what Pastor Jennings was about to say.
I shivered to think that he would tell us
That you were going away.

But then he blessed us with the announcement
That your service has expanded.
What happiness and joy came over me;
I could hardly stand it.

You are a true servant of God dear George;
And it is plain for all to see.
You are genuine, kind, and compassionate,
And as dedicated as one can be.

So go forth as God has commissioned you;
And keep your service true.
Pastor Jennings could never have found
A more deserving servant than you.

Congratulations, and may God continue to guide
you in thoughts, words, and deeds; that you will
continue to be a blessing to Pastor Jennings, the
Grace Emmanuel Family, the Flint Community, the
State of Michigan, the United States of America,
and the World at large.
God bless and keep you in His loving care.

A BRAND NEW START

As different as night and day we are,
And yet we are the same.
Our Father in Heaven says we are;
And His word I will proclaim.

And though we sometimes disagree,
And see things from different points of view;
We are still sisters in the Lord;
And that seals my love for you.

I prayed for God's will, not mine, to be done,
And He told me what to do.
He told me that He loves us both,
And His word is always true.

I asked Him to renew my mind,
And give me a brand new heart.
And now I say to you dear friend
We must make a brand new start.

May you be blessed beyond measure,
And God keep you in His loving care.

158

FRIENDS ARE FOREVER

When hearts are joined together,
And a true friendship has begun;
The bond cannot be broken,
And remains bright like the noonday sun.

It is my firm belief my friend,
That true friendship never ends.
The most vicious storm, nor the sharpest sword,
Can pierce the hearts of friends.

Although our paths now seldom cross,
And we have gone our separate ways;
The memories of our friendship
Still linger, and brighten my days.

So please know my dear friend,
That you are forever in my prayers.
Yes, true friends are forever,
And no other bond compares.

May God's Blessings Encompass You Always

159

SOMETHING MISSING

A very vital part of my life is missing
As I go about my daily tasks.
So I prayed to God for guidance,
And this is what I asked:

I asked Him to let His will be done,
And keep us in His care.
I asked Him to direct our paths,
And deliver us from despair.

He took me to Ephesians 4:31-32,
And made it very clear;
That it grieves His Holy Spirit,
When true friendships disappear.

He showed me what is missing,
And His words rang clear and true;
That the vital part that is missing,
My dear friend, is YOU.

So I penned these words to let you know
That you are loved unconditionally;
And still very dear to my heart,
As you will be eternally.

May God grant us the spirit of forgiveness,
And keep us in His care always.

IV

Christmas in Rhyme

The birth of our Lord and Savior, Jesus Christ, is without exception the greatest cause for celebration. It is because of His coming that we have hope for tomorrow. He is worthy to be praised. The following expressions in honor of our Savior are the result of my concern that we must never forget or ignore THE REASON FOR THE SEASON.

THE REASON FOR THE SEASON

The reason for the season is Jesus;
And to celebrate His love;
To tell the world of His goodness,
And to focus on His Kingdom above.

There is peace and joy all around us,
As we sing and praise His name.
The reason for this blessed season,
Is to let His praises ring.

When we make a joyful noise,
And give honor to our King;
The reason for the season,
Can be heard in the songs we sing.

So be blessed our dear friend...
And look up to heaven above.
May God always bless and keep you,
And shower you with His love.

OUR WISH FOR YOU

May the joy of the Christmas season,
Fill your hearts with joyous peace;
And encompass you throughout the year,
With blessings that never cease.

May you feel the presence of our Lord,
As He blesses you from day to day;
And be surrounded by His goodness,
As you travel along your way.

May your mornings be made brighter,
By the sweetness of birds in song;
And you take time to smell the roses,
As you remember to whom you belong.

And as you celebrate this special time,
May you remember God's sacrifice;
And that the reason for this joyous season,
Is our Lord and Savior, Jesus Christ.

Merry Christmas

THE JOY OF CHRISTMAS I

Christmas is very special;
The celebration of our Savior's birth.
No other season is so joyous,
In heaven or in earth.

The angels sing with gladness,
And stars shine brightly from above;
At the entrance of God's precious son,
To shower us with His love.

Oh what a joyous occasion!
No other can compare;
Except His second coming,
When we behold Him in the air.

May The Joy Of Christmas Be Yours
And The New Year Showered With Blessings.

THE JOY OF CHRISTMAS II

May the joy of the Christmas season,
Be yours throughout the year;
And the love of God embrace you,
And always hold you near.

Jesus, our Lord and Savior,
Is on whom we must concentrate.
His birth, death, and resurrection,
Gave us much to celebrate.

May your ministry be filled with blessings,
As you celebrate our Lord;
And the blessed Christmas season,
Bring you joy and sweet rewards.

May your days be filled with cheer;
And your lives be blessed abundantly,
As you praise God throughout the year.

Have A Merry Christmas And A Happy New Year

A PASTOR'S PRAYER

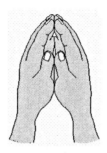

May the joy of the Christmas season
Be yours throughout the year.
May our Savior look down upon you,
And keep you in His loving care.

May you continue to receive the anointing
To preach and teach God's holy word.
May His arms embrace you gently,
And your peace is never disturbed.

May god shed His light upon you;
And bless you to do His will.
May you walk closely in His footsteps,
And to temptations, never yield.

May your faith in our blessed Savior
Grow stronger day by day;
And you receive enormous blessings,
In Jesus' name I pray.

V

My Daily Prayers

In conclusion, I have decided to share a few of my daily prayers in the hope that the reader will be inspired to trust that God loves us, and has provided each and every one with a spiritual gift. We are often unaware of our gifts, but if we but ask God for a revelation, He will surely enlighten us. It is then, our responsibility to use our gifts and talents in honor and praise of Him.

Thanks be to God, all honor, praise, and glory are yours forever and ever.

Amen.

MY DAILY PRAYER

Every morning when I rise,
I rededicate myself to thee.
I ask in the name of Jesus:
Help me to be what you want me to be.

Help me to walk in the path of righteousness,
And to praise you throughout this day.
Give me strength to defeat the enemy,
In his attempt to lead me astray.

Let my words be true and kind,
And my deeds the very same.
Let everything I do today,
Be in your precious name.

Let me disappoint the enemy Lord,
And bring a smile upon your face.
Let my worship and praise be real,
As I run this tedious race.

I thank you for your many blessings,
And I will not cease to pray;
And dedicate my life to you Lord,
As I die to self each day.

Bless us indeed Father, and deliver us from sin.
In Jesus' name.
Amen

MY FERVENT PRAYER

Father, help me to not offend you in any way.
Help me to please you in all I do and say.

Help me to remember that You are always near.
Even in my darkest hours, You will calm my every fear.

Deliver me from sin Lord, and keep me in your care.
Let the enemy not harm me, or cause me to despair.

Let your mercies shine around me,
And strengthen me to do your will.
Erase all doubts, and renew my mind,
And let your peace be still.

Increase my faith dear Lord, even when troubles rise.
Help me to remember your precious Son,
And keep my eyes on the prize.

Forgive my sins Heavenly Father,
And help me to make you smile.
Let me be a disappointment to the enemy,
And his reign be but for a little while.

Keep me close to you dear Lord.
Let me walk in your guiding light.
Never wavering in my faith and trust,
Until my soul takes flight.

Let me fly into your arms, and be caressed by your saving grace.
All my trials will be over, when I see your smiling face.

I ask it all in the name of your precious son Jesus.
Amen

BLESSED ASSURANCE
(Praise, Thanksgiving, & Petition)

Most gracious and merciful Father,
we thank you for your ever presence.
Even in times of sorrow and despair, You are there.
Help us to look beyond our earthly circumstances Lord;
and be filled with the joy of knowing and trusting you.

Help us Father, to be forever mindful
of your goodness and mercy;
and that no matter what the circumstances,
You are always in full control.

Thank you for loving and caring for us Lord,
in spite of our human frailties.
We ask that you cleanse us from all
unrighteousness.
Give us humble spirits Lord,
and let us do your will with vigor, and excitement.

Thank you for delivering us Lord, from sin,
and help us to live lives that are pleasing in your sight.
We ask it all in the precious name of Jesus.

Amen

MY REQUEST

Heavenly Father, I thank you for your goodness.
I ask that you strengthen me to conquer
all that would be displeasing to you.
Create in me a clean and pure heart Father.
Let there be no evil, wickedness, or deceit in me.
Let your Holy Spirit dwell in me.
Give me the joy and peace that comes from
knowing, loving, trusting, and obeying you.
Let me not be concerned about the temporal and material
things of this world Lord;
but to stay focused on the eternal things of your Kingdom.
Help me Father, to live in total honor and praise of you;
and to be a total disappointment to the enemy.
I ask it all in the precious name of my Savior Jesus Christ.

Amen

THANK YOU GOD

Almighty God, Creator of all that exist,
we thank you for all you have done for us.
Thank you Father God for your son Jesus.
Thank you Jesus, for your love and sacrifice.
Thank you for your Holy Spirit.
Thank you Father God, for the desire to please you.
Thank you for the air we breathe,
the food we eat, the sounds we hear, the aromas we smell,
the sights we see, and the love we feel.
Thank you Master, for your gift of salvation.
We thank You.
We praise You.
We worship You.
Hallelujah, Hallelujah
Amen

Prayer I

Thank you Heavenly Father, for the gift of poetic expression. Let me use your gift in honor and praise of you always. Let the words of my mouth, and the meditations of my heart, be acceptable in your sight. Let my thoughts, words, and deeds, be pleasing to you Lord. I thank you for all you have done, and all you plan to do in my life. Help me to seek and do your will and not my own Lord. Let this book of poetry and expressions from my heart, be a blessing to all who read it. I hereby give you all the honor, all the glory and all the praise. I commit to your will Lord, and ask that you bless me in deed, increase my territory, and keep your hands on me so that I do no evil or cause any pain. I ask it all in the name of your precious son Jesus.

Amen.

Prayer II

Thank you Father God, for your son Jesus, who is our hope for tomorrow and always. Thank you for your Holy Spirit, who comforts, leads, and guides me. I trust you Father God, because I believe you alone are Lord, and most high in all the universe. I have hope for tomorrow because of your gift of salvation through your son Jesus. I feel your love all around me Father, and I see your works. I ask that you continue to strengthen me to do your will, and to please you in all I do and say, I ask you to forgive my sins and strengthen me to forgive those who trespass against me. Let your spirit live inside of me Lord, and let my life reflect your goodness always. Let my praise and worship be real Lord. I ask it all in the precious name of Jesus.

Amen

173

Prayer III

Thank you God, for the miracles that only you can create; the flowers, the sun, the moon, the stars, the skies, the mountains, the rivers, the streams, the rain, the snow, the cool breezes, the green grass, the birds, the butterflies, the world, and all that is within. Let me focus on your creations in times of trouble. Help me to make the best of whatever life brings, knowing what is important is your love for me, and your grace and mercy. Help me laugh and love more; to be more kind, giving, and forgiving. Let my thoughts be pure and my deeds be kind, keep me in your care, and help me to look beyond the evils of this world. In Jesus name I pray.

Amen

Prayer IV

Thank you Father God, Jesus, and Holy Spirit, for the joy of knowing you. Strengthen me in your will Lord, and let me feel the love, peace, and joy that only comes from you. Let my whole being stay focused on you, so that the evils and wickedness of this world cannot steal or disturb my joy. My joy comes from knowing you Lord; and knowing that you are always near. Let me not be distracted by material things. Let my eyes seek your glory; my ears hear and understand your words; my heart feel your presence; my tongue praise your name; my nostrils breathe your spirit, and smell the sweetness of your goodness. You are my joy Lord. Please keep me in your loving care. In Jesus' name I pray.

Amen

VI

A Final Word

This final expression was inspired by a very trying and stressful day in the Emergency Room on the first day of Spring.

SEASONAL REALITY
(In The E.R.)

First day of Spring
would normally bring joyous applause,
if not for the havoc of restless souls coming to life
after mounds of snow, ice, slippery roads, and
involuntary confinement.
Oh how those restless souls go wild after the hibernation of winter.
Hotrods roll, young girls stroll,
young boys go packing, with good judgment lacking;
showing off their pieces with little concern for consequences.
Ambulances screaming and speeding
to this, my place, my calling.
Horns spouting in-coming disasters,
And teams getting ready for life saving battles.
Run Social Worker! Run!
Make haste to console the weeping
mothers, fathers, sisters, brothers, wives, children, and friends
of ones whose lives may well be ending.
Why? How? Where? When? Who?
Unanswered questions with no answers in sight.
Lives slipping away like thieves in the night.
Blood curding screams from those left behind.
Oh, if the beauty of Spring would only trigger Godly things.
Pray, pray, pray for better days;
when young men no longer glory in mischievous things.
When excitement comes from church bells ringing,
Birds chirping, flowers blooming, stars twinkling,
And choirs singing songs of love.
When will we learn that LOVE is the key to all that is good?
Not until then will we all be set free
from the evils of the enemy, who steals our joy
If we fail to hold fast to the teachings of our Lord.
Let us enjoy the beauty of Spring,

And put away all those evil things;
the guns, the knives, the booze and drugs.
Let us hold fast to the power of LOVE,
And be women and men of God, for ALL SEASONS

To Contact The Author

Visit her website at www.lpexpressions.com
Or email: lailai1044@comcast.net

TO ORDER COPIES OF SAYING IT WITH POETRY
PLEASE FILL OUT THIS ORDER FORM

NAME_____

ADDRESS_____

CITY_____STATE_____ZIPCODE_____

PHONE _____EMAIL_____

Check below to place your order

Qty.

_____Saying It With Poetry $16.00 per copy   _____

_____other_____

Make all checks or money orders payable to Ladalia Postell
(add .06 cent sales tax on the dollar+$2 for (S&H).
Clip and mail to

Ladalia Postell
329 Allendale Pl.
Flint, MI 48503

178

NOTES

Printed in the United States
34310LVS00005B/79-558

9 780976 964520